The Skin we Breathe

*Poetry
&
Photography*

KIANA ANGALIA

Zerzura Studios

Words, Photography & Design
by Kiana Angalia

kianaangalia.com

follow the visual story on instagram:
kiana.angalia.poetry
kiana.angalia.art

for stories exploring the resilience of the human spirit
listen to the Emergence podcast.

Published by *Zerzura Studios*
Woodstock, New York

ISBN: 978-91-987108-2-3

The Skin
we Breathe

Poetry
&
Photography

KIANA ANGALIA

for Moana

i'll see you on the other side,
wait for me there.

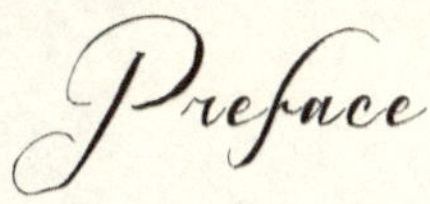# Preface

This book is for Moana. One of my dearest friends, who passed away to cancer in April 2022. Even though I may never be able to read this to you, I like to believe you hear these poems as I speak them into the air. For on some level, I know you are listening.

Parts of you will always remain embedded beneath this skin and in the parts of my heart where the light lives. Because people like you don't fade. Oh my dear, *you echo on —*

Your warmth and your energy feels as real and alive as the day I met you. That misted afternoon on the highest floors of the hospital. When you walked in with the chemo stand in hand and I recognized you instantly, because you shone so bright. It was a sisterhood at first sight. Something that lives on. And how we painted our bare heads red with henna and laughed because we knew we wore crowns all along, despite the tubes that flowed from our veins and our beautiful ageless faces. The chemo that doused our minds and gave us lurid gazes and our smiles had to try so hard to break through. But with you, it was always easy. Because that is who you were.

Moana, my darling, I am deeply grateful for our extraordinary friendship. You will always be one of the brightest stars in my sky before I sleep. No one may fully understand what we have been through. What you have been through. But I am in wonder of you, and of it all —

Kiana Angalia
6th May 2022
Woodstock, New York

Also by Kiana Angalia

Emergence

Untethered

Red Ambrosia

Zerzura Studios

The Skin
we Breathe

Poetry
&
Photography

KIANA ANGALIA

i wish you were here to read this.
but i like to think
traces of these words
float so high
that when i breathe them into the night sky,
even you can feel them.

you opened a portal
to that room with no doors.
we grew there
in that sterile place where nothing else grows
where plants perish at the scent
but we grew
out of there —

you grew so high
that you left
even me behind.

every night
and every morning
i read a poem for her

dozens of recorded voice messages
so that when she'd wake
and drift to sleep
she might have something to hold on to
to take with her, into that other place —

for she is dying
and this is the best way i know how
to say
how much i love her.

The Orchard

in times i could not move
i would dream of peaches.

i would watch her delight, lick her lips
as yellow dribbled down her mouth & laugh
i caught it from the window
and taste peaches through her

my mouth was an open wound
but i could imagine as far
i sailed on her laughter
transported to the orchard where they grew
even though i drank dark green liquid through a tube

for a moment i was taken there
somewhere filled with verdant air —
orchards of southern France
a place i would one day return
sit amidst the orchard, buzzing & in bloom

& how it tastes all the richer
because of what we have been through.

Seasons

i am not the old me
who clung to seasons
of fertility
in fear they may not return

now i rest in inevitable unfolding
as my wings sway
in patience, knowing
it takes winter and seasons
to digest
all the fruits of summer.

Part II

i am not the old me
who wanders aimless
in search for belonging
in longing for something more.

i wander still
but now i live
within this pulsing chamber
behind my ribs
where sleeping words lie.

winter feels empty without her
but when i allow myself to *feel* —
buds grow into the hollow spaces she left

maybe i shall meet her again someday
in a different time
when i am old
and she is young
in a different body than the one she left behind

will we recognize each other then?
wearing different skin suits
speaking in different tongues
one of us old and the other young

it may never be the same
but the connection we made
breaches the continents of time.

The Skin We Breathe

Kiana Angalia

poetry filters
through her dreams
when she wakes
she is afraid to speak
lest they disappear
into the atmosphere

so she sleeps
with ink & paper
beside her bed
and when words slip through
to her consciousness
she transfers their tangled patterns
letting blood & ink weave together
what in waking day
she could not remember.

be gentle with the world
she has soft edges when you let her
corners are not really corners
just swerves in a different direction

-what winter taught me

the direction we move
depends on whether
we let
fear
or love
guide the way —

hate is too heavy to carry
and i still have a ways to go
on my journey home.

Kiana Angalia

13

in the beginning
when you told me winter
was your favourite season
i didn't understand.
but when i walked with you
through november
and all her snowy days
that too made sense

for she made the world clear again
she made the world transparent

and even though that was years ago,
our memories are planted like smooth stones in
my pocket,
the ones i left at home.
and every now and then
i catch a glimmer of winter sun on snow
i see what you saw, standing there looking out
the window
at birds dancing on fallen snow.

Kiana Angalia

in the beginning
when you told me winter
was your favourite season
i didn't understand.
but when i walked with you
through november
and all her snowy days
that too made sense

for she made the world clear again
she made the world transparent

and even though that was years ago,
our memories are planted like smooth stones in
my pocket,
the ones i left at home.
and every now and then
i catch a glimmer of winter sun on snow
i see what you saw, standing there looking out of
the window
at birds dancing on fallen snow.

Every time you fall
i will be here
sitting on the floor
beside you.

i will be here
till we rise together
as the moon rises through the night
no matter how dark it is.

The Darkest Phases
Lead us
To the Lightest Places

Kiana Angalia

All has fallen
to the ground it rests
how beautiful our winter was
a season i will never forget.

the desert strips us bare
there's nothing we can hide here
it brings us to the end of things
an end is an end
            is a beginning —

i am coming back to the surface
here,
      writing, and living

this — *is breathing*

writing, is breathing

    -after a long winter

The Endurance of a Heartbeat

it was there —
your heartbeat
my pen
writing down the edges of our reality

and i will continue to do so
long after
you are gone.

thank goddess my pen
has the endurance
of a heartbeat

she carries me on —

she sits by the fountain
reading books
i wrote, lifetimes ago.

seeing her reading my heart
keeps me going,
            to this day.

i gaze at her for a moment longer
       she doesn't even know my name.

come to my house
i have great books
for us to read and to wear
when we are lonely, naked and aware
that we are not the only ones
longing
for something we cannot quite put words to.

Kiana Angalia

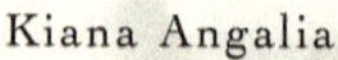

Birds on snow

we loved to watch birds
dance on snow
from our hospital window
we would delight
all the more
because we were trapped
inside

they'd flutter and dance,
and taste the sun
on their wings for us.

it never works —
pushing, force, pressure
is the best way
to destroy ourselves
and each other

the greatest power
is held in the wings of gentleness

we sit outside
in the still company of winter
steam pours from her lips
as she sips
hot tea
and winter hugs us closer

she traces her fingers
on the frosted table
his name, the one she left behind
the one she let herself free from

she says it was the poetry
the writing that gave her permission
to let her wings unfold

On the other side

my best friend
is dying
she has
a few months
no one knows
how many
or how much
opioids
she will have to take
to keep on

words leave me
when i think of her
and try to remember
that she is only leaving for a while
and that i will see her
soon again
on the other side.

death,
when walked with grace
slips us silently
back into the undergrowth
to the place
from whence we all came

i met her before the scent of rain
she told me it was on its way
i didn't believe her
but held her hand anyway

and when rain falls on our shoulders
i held her into the sun —

sunshine brings
expectations.
rain brings
poetry.

i always liked rainy days.

Kiana Angalia

the world has turned
to shades of grey
i have nothing left to say
she is gone
i am empty
all the poems i wanted to share
will forever remain
on my lips.
all that i still wanted
to show her
rests
forever embedded
in these palms
empty & open
to death
to dust
with dreams and songlines
and everything i thought i once knew

the poems that resonate the most
are the lines which feel
as if they were my own.

ah, it is as if i wrote this!
and in a way we did
because this is *our* story
it emerges —
from the spaces between us
the woven seams of human
relationships that fold across time

and when meaning is ready to be born
it finds a willing mind
to absorb and refine
put out into the world
for someone else to find

and see, *ah! this is but my own!*
this poem, i already know.

poetry is words beyond language
for we must understand
the depths of ourselves first
to feel poetry
echo back to us
beyond words
what we don't quite —
yet already,
know

it is hard
to let my head down
and rest
when i know
i have to rise again and face
all i wanted to fade away.

when despair rises
when it barrels through
my stomach my liver

when i feel helpless,
enter me
at loss,
move through me —
i want to know who lives here
truly, who knocks at the door

let me in
so i may sleep while you lie awake
and watch, while you sleep
candlelight, ink smudged in places
always on your hands, even the half-eaten peach
holds your mark
on me
on tomorrow

cradle me for now
don't leave me yet in this crevice
with my heart
full of sorrow.

what if the parts we lost
along the way
are waiting for us

patiently waiting
for a place we can get to within ourselves
to welcome them home again.

singing softly from outer space;
i knew you would come,
i knew you would

and when you are ready
i will be waiting there.

may i die
with an open book on my chest
and my palms wide open to the sky
gazing into the distance
with a softness
and knowing
that i am coming home.

back to literature,
when all else
has gone astray.

Kiana Angalia

her mouth breathes warm words into the night air
she was sitting out on the pier
i couldn't hear her
but i felt her words all the way through.

-*stories told from heart*

The Skin We Breathe

how do i reach into a pool of water?
when i hesitate to interrupt
the stillness preserved on its surface

Kiana Angalia

tubes cascade like waterfalls
from every hollow, beam and force —
their way through this skin

these plastic portal veins
i cannot tell what is me
anymore

extending into the peripheries
of this hospital room
these steril edges
these dampened ledges

does this eye
see clearly enough?
or must i learn the truth
from different a place
find my way around this house
all over again

uncovering, letting go
of yesterday and tomorrow

ask questions
to the universe and her fractaled parts
they will answer,
perhaps they too
are only seeking their way
back to each other.

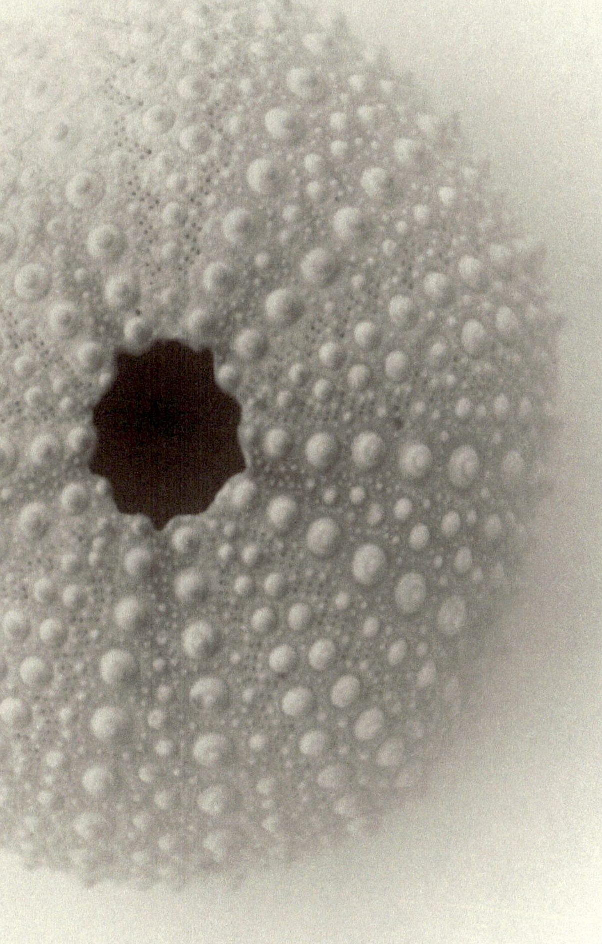

embrace of solitude
holds a space
in heart
my crowded mind
never could.

she makes the world a blank slate
clean again
each phase is a beginning
where i don't need anything

i enjoy her glittering company
and how she makes me feel
at home within myself.

-*snow*

On Loneliness

loneliness is like glancing through a window
into the vacant rooms of one's soul. it is the
feeling of hollow. a loss of belonging to one-
self. and because of that, struggling to find
meaning. a train to nowhere.

but nowhere is nowhere is somewhere
somewhere,
     there must be something there —

The Skin We Breathe

Vienna

am i allowed to cry here?
these streets held me captive
for such a long while. i am bound to them.
this place saved me —
even when i did not want it to
Vienna, forgive me if i am not as immaculate as you

you held me when i fell through
three times
we died in you

Vienna,
you are my end,
> *and my beginning —*

indulge in the vernacular
of the places you place
your feet
learn her roots and her seedlings
the angle her web spreads forth —
her song and — *how here*
do the birds wake me at dawn?
how here —
does the rain smell as it falls
to the forest floor
the sky in my teacup
her scent, as i sip her
all the way home
the knowing and the unknown
walking the unfamiliar road
everything, perhaps,
is a journey home.

A ∂ance of water

do you know the magic of water?
as it dances in ripples
to some far off tune

the glider adds to it
skimming across the surface
of what we cannot see

and salmon,
as she rises her head
to peek into the world
she rests beneath

or when water skirts
over the edge of a rock blade
taking all my expectations
down with it

here is the ∂ance of water
here is the ∂ance of life

Kiana Angalia

what a relief
to know
that life
is harder on us
than death.

she walks the beach alone
in search of driftwood
casting memories away
in exchange for pieces carved out by the sea.
i wonder if she still holds in her hand,
the quiet memories of me.

he sits on a stone, outside an old bookstore
of course i walked up to him
and asked what he did on a seat like that
with a view of the acropolis and his paints
he said he translates songs
and watches how history mixes with modern times
through his paints and colours.

when the end comes
i wish to have tapped into the wonders
to have eavesdropped on the stars
as they cast their melodies
across the arcs of the cosmos
and whisper stories
of the patterns
woven through eternity.

the way we treat her
is in essence
the way we are treating ourselves

-*nature*

Surrender

a part of me has always longed to surrender
to fall gently
back into the ocean
how she knows how to hold us
naturally, as water does
like womb, before birth.

i lean towards gentle things
softness,
the relief that night sky brings
how she expects nothing from me
because she contains everything
in the vastness
of herself.

i lean towards the gentle things
soft skin that receives mine
with a knowing
we both belong here.

maybe we need this winter
of death & disarray
for everything to peel away
to learn to harmonize our confusion
to listen to what our body
and soul
wants to say.

when i am lost
looking for a new path
i close my eyes
and follow
the soft pulse
of this beating heart,
it seems she is the only one
who knows her way
through the dark.

Kiana Angalia

i wait for her to rise
fire, air, water
the spirit, the holy mother
she knows
how to move here
she teaches, *listen* —
hold shell to ear
let filter in stories from the ocean
we are endlessly arriving
at the shores of ourselves

perpetually uncovering
rediscovering
the stories that live inside
the parts that silently speak
through Einaudi's melodies
ruffling across the strings of soul
playing the sound of eternity.

skin abraised and wounded
to heal, they tell me,
we are doing this to heal
what lies beneath your skin you cannot see
the truth of
—feel, can you feel me?

even when i lie beneath these bedsheets
white for my eyes to paint
with sunsets of distant places
take me upwards
through memories of faded spaces
that make up stargates
of my imagination

i soar —
uncaptured here

she feels the tangled spindles
wrapped inside her cheekbone
a carpet of cells
there to bring her deeper
into the caverns of herself

and at this age
it is known
when she declares,
i never needed you
or anyone else
to protect me from myself.

Kiana Angalia

The Taste of Snow

we would delight
in the taste of snow
knowing, we may not be there
to feel it melt on our tongues
tomorrow

he always enjoyed yawning.
and years later i understood,
perhaps it is a *settling in*
an acceptance
that we do not know everything

regard!
    the joy in simple things

what if flowers could sing
hold my hand and dance
along the peripheries
of circles in mind
walk alongside me for a while
as i wander across the river

i have always enjoyed the company of lilies
their self-assured wisdom
wildflowers, and how they sing with the wind
lilacs in their silent reverie
and the regal company of roses.

never doubting
they belong here.

*are we the only species
that question our belonging?*

Kiana Angali

Cape Jasmine

you are my song of winter
when i breathe the shallow plume
thoughts of you
glide upon the scented air
of cape jasmine waiting to bloom
as spring arrives
and the becoming of anew

i will let myself out
of this cage
through the back door
as everything i thought i wanted
i need no more

let parts die
as a thousand snowflakes fall
back into the snow.

All things die in solitude.

Part I

she holds her poems to the air
transparent for sky to breathe
to lull and imbue
drench and delight
in the taste of poetry

Part II

she holds her poems
up for the sky to see
does this poem breathe?
does she have wings
that dapper through the reader's mind
or does it never quite let lift
fall flat, trodden over by the bends of time.

sky, will you teach me
how to fly these poems higher?

Kiana Angalia

i relish in this
soft silence
like milk blue sky
and misted morning hue

the greatest gift
is that at the end of the day
i rest in knowing
there is always someone
to come home to.

-what family means

it is okay
to sit and wait
for the beginnings of tomorrow
when your mind is empty
and your heart full of sorrow.

sadness opens
hollow wells within me
to let water and air
flow through

these days, i appreciate the silence
when once it felt lonely.
now, it gives space to breathe
as i write melodies through —

⎯

give her a silver nugget
an empty walnut shell
and she will whisper a poem in your ear
in exchange for what you see and hear.

Kiana Angalia

i will never sacrifice
the quality of the life i am living
for an extended segment of brittle linear time
i wish to live fully —
and when the time comes to transition
i will be standing at the doorway
ready, for whatever meets me there.

the moon. whose relationship with earth pulls
in the reins of change itself. while she sits and
watches, in a way where patience is no thing. all
she does is breathe. drawing us in and letting us
go with each of her breaths. pulling the oceans
with her. moving the cycles of time.

home, she whispers,
always, we are on our way home.

i grew an arm
in healing the relationship with my sister
as if a part of me was missing
for so long, i forgot how it felt like
to reach her.

these nights, i leave my windows open
for the breeze to slip through
along with thoughts and memories of you

may the wind
always carry you
with her

so that when i feel her tickled whisper
i know, you are there
with us too.

in empty streets
i find my voice
in empty streets
i fill my trough
of water and of peace of mind
let me wander these empty streets through time.

how to be —
with this emptiness inside
the sphere where all things arise
and dip silently in
and out of sight
as with the stars
and our moon
across the velvet skies.

-when we remember

Kiana Angalia

sleeping beneath abandoned ruins
seeing the world through a shepherds eyes
what a tranquil life, it must be
old walls that hold stories of heart
the ones we cycle and weave
as we sleep, amongst the quiet leaves
to the sound of tides running
on the periphery of our dreams
weaving another verse
together
through sleep.

in these places
no one, and everyone
belongs

Kiana Angalia

Kiana Angalia

The knife

where has she reached into
what depths has she kissed
with her tip, her shimmer, her width

who has she broken *open* —
tell me your stories
who you have split
who you have touched
who you have marked and kissed
with your assured belonging

daring us to reach further —
into our organs and beneath them
into all the hidden spaces
that live within

and all that you bring
the beginning and the end
the quiet kiss of death.

The Skin We Breathe

she dwells in the house of writing. life is a dash-
ing tumultuous storm. writing, it seems, is the only
adequate interpreter. writing allows us to to see
through the looking glass. to wipe away the mist.
to witness the underbelly.
to wander through —
to partake
& cocreate
in life —
and her boundless mystery.

The Skin We Breathe

do traces of us linger quietly in the air?
and when i walk past the place you once
stood,
is a part of you still there?

i like to believe,
traces of us hover and vibrate
throughout eternity
even though, that is far beyond
what i may ever know.

when you ask what my name is
what i do for a living
what i have done
where i am from
—there lies no energy there
nothing waits to burst open

Ask instead —
what currents move me
what shifts the mind
from dark to light
where i go to play with shadows
what i see between moss and vine
bough and forest floor
where i dance with wolves and starlight
in search for evermore —

kinder days arise
from the ashes
when we let it burn
to the ground.

-the importance of death

Ocean of Solitude

she sits in quiet solitude
as if she had always been there
gulls speak for her
she needs no voice here

to hear beneath it all
the space where stillness lives
moans and tumbles her thoughts like the sea
even in solitude we bear fragments of another
and i am ever wandering
till she returns back to me.

words land softly by her feet
they sit at the edge of her bed
waiting for her to wake
to the taste of them
to bring them down to the sea
let them soak in cool water
lull beside her feet.
and here she releases
her memories
back into the sea

The Empty Shoreline

she writes poetry
on chards of paper
tucks it in a bottle
and lets it out to sea.

he walks along the shoreline
murmuring his living, the water beckoning,
beckoning —
how much easier it would be, to leave

he glances at the bottle
sees the russell inside
opens up the paper
and takes in the lines

they tell of a girl who nearly left
but wrote it down & out,
and as ink bled on paper
gained back her life instead

he reaches in his pocket
and pulls out a pen
sets the ink to paper
and remembers
all he has left

salt from his eyes
meet the salted sea
he writes;
somtimes it feels like there is nothing left for
me,
it would be easier to give in to the ocean.

but the string of words
wrap around his wrist
the ones she whispered
out into the wind

he turns towards the sea
resting her words in mind
walks back up the shoreline
and chooses to stay alive.

Kiana Angalia

Death of Young Poets

write what you can
before you run —
out
    of
        time

poets die young. they say
and we don't need to look far to see it

Plath, Wheatley, Keats, & Brontë,
Plath at her own hands, Keats to disease and
Gillespie Magee who fell from the sky

all into the arms of death

yet these are the people who changed the world
their words ring out
across the bands of time
rippling through generations
ushering us into the coming phases
urging us gently on —

poetry is never lost
it reverberates far beyond
the extent of our own lives.

Be courageous. Be kind.
And embrace it all —

Love,

Kiana Angalia

Photographs in this book were taken by Kiana Angalia in Kenya, Austria, Sweden, France, Spain, Florida, British Columbia, New York, & Massachusetts.

with gratitude

I am deeply grateful to the humans and animals who walk beside me on this wild journey.

To Moana, for our extraordinary friendship. For everything we learnt together and all the adventures we shared.

To Ule, Thomas, Jona, Christoph, & Inga, for being the supportive & amazing family to Moana & for our adventures in Kenya.

To my father, who made it possible for Moana to visit Kenya for a precious few weeks. And to Doris, Eva & everyone at Moringa House for assisting with this.

To the doctors, nurses, therapists, & medical staff who carried us through these years.

To my mother, for your endless emotional support through everything.

I love you all.

ABOUT THE AUTHOR

Kiana Angalia is a writer, artist, photographer & explorer. She was born in Sweden & grew up in East Africa. Kiana is a three time cancer thriver. Although cancer left her with one eye, scars and facial differences, she is grateful for these experiences as they have led her on a profound journey of growth and self-discovery. She longs to empower others to dare to speak their truth, to share their stories and invite the world to see. Her work explores the continuous journey of healing, expansion, and what it means to embrace the vastness of this extraordinary human experience. She is a nomad at heart and lives between Kenya, Vienna, Amsterdam & New York.

kianaangalia.com | zerzurastudios@gmail.com.
@kiana.angalia.poetry & kiana.angalia.art
Podcast: Emergence

Words, Photography & Design
by Kiana Angalia